Alphabet *of*
SPACE

by Laura Gates Galvin   Illustrated by Higgins Bond

For my nephews, Jack and Charlie, who mean the world to me.—L.G.G.

This is for my two "out of this world" nephews, Jason and Kalel Higgins.—H.B.

Book copyright © 2006 Trudy Corporation
and Smithsonian Institution, Washington, DC 20560.

Published by Soundprints, an imprint of Trudy Corporation, Norwalk, Connecticut.
www.soundprints.com

Book design: Marcin D. Pilchowski
Editors: Barbie H. Schwaeber and Ben Nussbaum

First Edition 2006
10 9 8 7 6 5 4 3 2
Printed in China

Acknowledgments:
    Our very special thanks to Roger D. Launius of the National Air & Space Museum, Smithsonian Institution.
    Soundprints would also like to thank Ellen Nanney and Katie Mann at Smithsonian Institution's Office of
Product Development and Licensing for their help in the creation of this book.

Library of Congress Cataloging-in-Publication Data

Galvin, Laura Gates

    Alphabet of space / by Laura Gates Galvin ; edited by Ben Nussbaum.—1st ed.
        p. cm.—(Smithsonian alphabet books)
    ISBN 1-59249-656-3 (hardcover)
    1. Astronautics—Juvenile literature. 2. Alphabet books—Juvenile
literature. I. Nussbaum, Ben. II. Title. III. Series.
TL793.G324 2006
629.4—dc22
                                2006014813

Alphabet *of*
SPACE

by Laura Gates Galvin   Illustrated by Higgins Bond

Soundprints

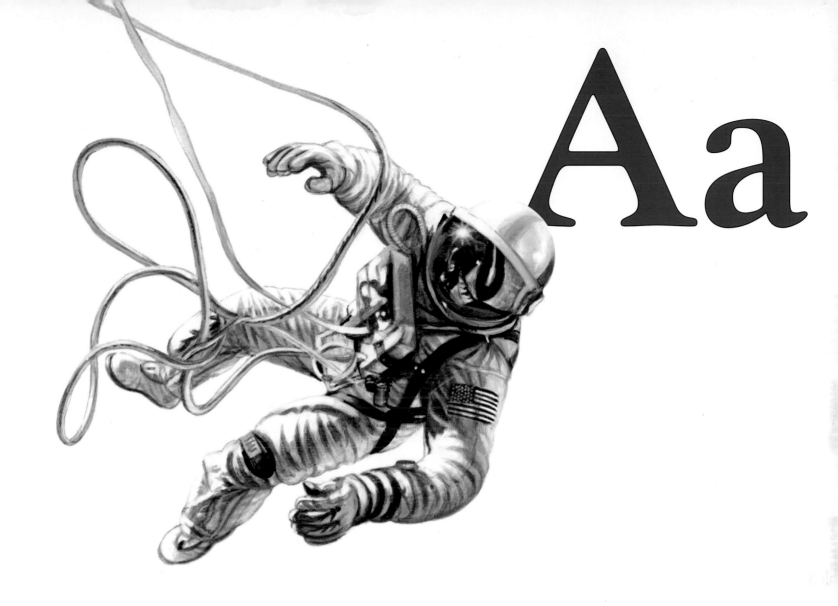

Aa

A is for **astronauts**
dressed in space suits,
with life support packs,
helmets, gloves and space boots.

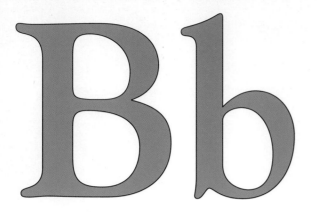

Bb

B is for **binoculars**.
You can see the stars—
gaze at the moon
and maybe see Mars!

Cc

C is for **comet**,
a bright object in the sky.
It's made of dust and ice.
Have you seen one streaking by?

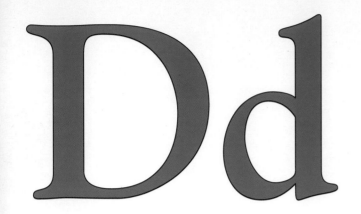

Dd

D is for **dwarf stars**.
They're not very bright.
Most can't be seen
even on a clear night.

E is for **Earth**
millions of miles from the sun.
It's the planet where we live,
eat, sleep, work and have fun!

Ee

Ff

F is for **full moon**,
big, round and bright.
Once every month
it lights up the night.

Gg

G is for **gravity**
causing things to fall down.
There's no gravity in space
so things float all around.

Hh

H is for **Hubble Telescope,**
a famous satellite.
It circles the earth
all day and all night.

Ii

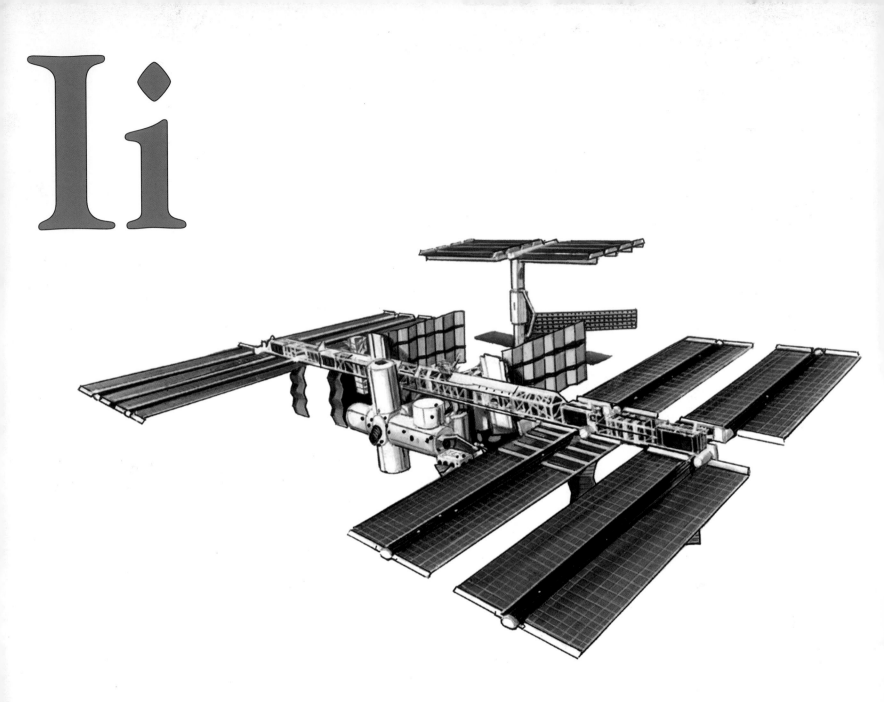

I is for **ISS**,
largest of all space stations.
A project led by the U.S.
and supported by many nations.

J j

J is for **Jupiter**
which is not at all small.
It's a very big planet—
the biggest planet of all.

Kk

K is for **Kepler.**
He discovered some rules—
like the movement of planets—
that are now taught in schools.

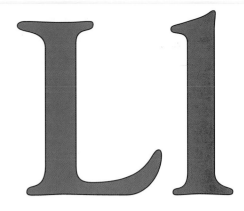

L is for **Lunar Rover**.
It served a great purpose.
The astronauts drove it
on the moon's surface.

Mm

M is for **Mars**
a planet that's red.
There's no life on Mars
or so it is said!

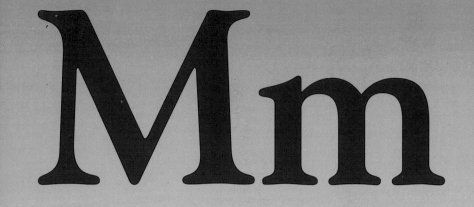

Nn

N is for **Neptune**
colored deep, shiny blue.
It has white streaky clouds
and a Great Dark Spot, too.

Oo

O is for **observatory**
a place for stargazing.
If you look through the telescope
what you'll see is amazing!

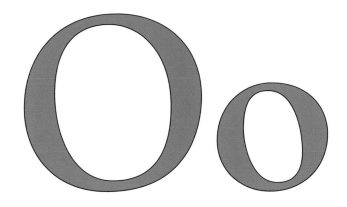

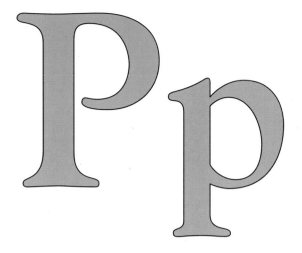

P is for **payload specialist**,
a spacecraft guest—
not always an astronaut,
but a trained scientist.

Qq

Q is for **quasars**,
the most intense source of light.
Billions of light-years from Earth
and unbelievably bright!

Rr

R is for **rocket**.
It's an absolute must
to launch a spacecraft
with its powerful thrust.

Ss

S is for **Saturn**
surrounded by shimmer.
When the rings that surround it
catch sunlight and glimmer.

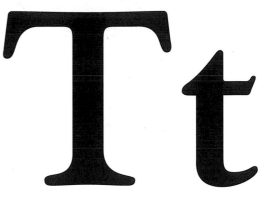

Tt

T is for **telescope**.
It makes planets look clear.
Although they are far,
they look very near.

Uu

U is for **U.S. moon landing**.
In the year 1969
man walked on the moon
for the very first time.

V v

V is for **Venus**
a planet that's far.
It is very bright
and shines like a star.

W is for **white dwarf star**.
Most are not very bright,
but one called Eradani
can be seen in the night.

Xx

X is for **X-15**.
It's impressive indeed.
It holds the record
for winged-aircraft speed!

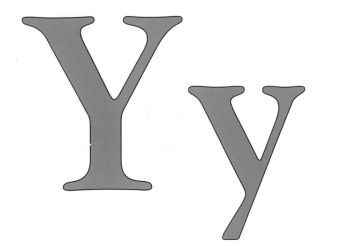

Y is for **year**.
When one year is done
the earth will have traveled
once 'round the sun.

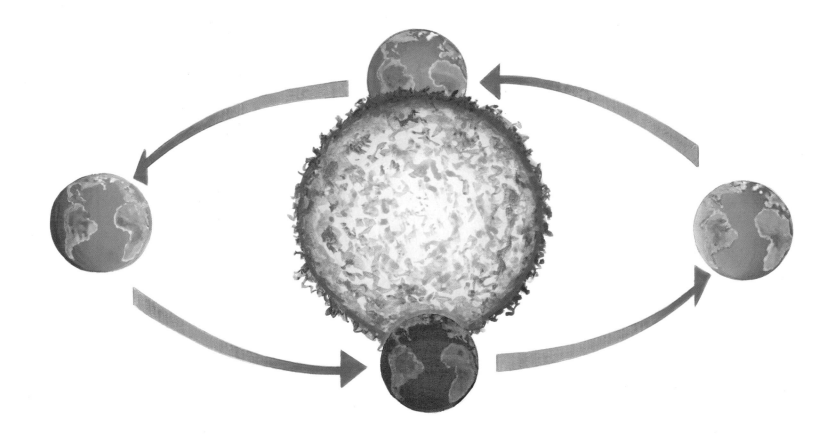

Z is for **zenith**,
a point way up high,
directly above us
far up in the sky.

GLOSSARY

ASTRONAUTS: The term "astronaut" comes from the Greek for "space sailor," and refers to the people who are launched as crewmembers aboard NASA spacecraft bound for orbit and beyond. The first astronauts to walk on the moon were Neil Armstrong and Buzz Aldrin.

BINOCULARS: Binoculars make distant objects look larger and closer. Astronomers use binoculars and telescopes to study stars and planets. Binoculars are a good tool for amateurs to use to study the night sky.

COMET: Comets are bright objects with tails that can be seen streaking through the sky at night. They may look impressive, but they are really just balls of dirty ice measuring about one mile in length. The tail is formed when the sun begins to melt the ice. This is what can be seen in the sky: the sunlight catching the tail. Comets can be seen when they travel close to the sun. Some comets can reach speeds of over one million miles per hour when they are traveling near the sun.

DWARF STARS: Dwarf stars are relatively small stars. There are different kinds of dwarf stars. Our sun is a yellow dwarf star. White dwarf stars are very, very dense and hot. Black dwarf stars are very small, cold, dead stars.

EARTH: Earth is the fifth largest planet in our solar system. Earth is made up mostly of rock and a core made up of nickel and iron. Earth is the only known planet that has water on its surface, which is one reason it is suitable for life. Over 70 % of the earth's surface is under water.

FULL MOON: The moon is full when it looks like a complete circle. A full moon occurs every month. The moon is called a crescent when it is shaped like a C, and the moon is called gibbous when it is not yet a full moon, but more than half of the moon is visible.

GRAVITY: Gravity is the pulling force that holds everything on the earth to the ground. Lack of gravity causes astronauts to float around their space cabin unless they are tied down.

HUBBLE TELESCOPE: The Hubble Telescope is a satellite in space. Space telescopes are very useful. Because they are in space, they have a better view of the solar system than planetary satellites. The Hubble Telescope was launched in 1990, but its main mirror had a spherical aberration when it was launched that made the images slightly fuzzy. In December 1993, astronauts inserted corrective electronics to overcome the defective mirror.

INTERNATIONAL SPACE STATION (ISS): The International Space Station (ISS) is the largest and most complex international scientific project in history. Led by the United States, the International Space Station draws upon the scientific and technological resources of Canada, Japan, Russia, the European Space Agency and Brazil.

JUPITER: Jupiter is the biggest planet in the solar system. It is twice as large as all the other planets put together. Jupiter has no surface for spacecraft to land on because it is mostly made up of helium gas and hydrogen. In 1995, the Galileo space probe reached Jupiter and its moon.

KEPLER, JOHANNES: Johannes Kepler was a German astronomer whose published explanation of planetary motion became known as Kepler's Laws.

LUNAR ROVER: The lunar rover was a vehicle used by astronauts to drive on the moon during the Apollo space program in the early 1970s. As with everything taken to the moon, weight and size were major considerations. The Lunar Rover was designed to fold up and attach to the side of the lunar lander.

MARS: Mars is called the red planet because of its rusty red color. The color comes from rusted iron in its soil. The Viking probes that reached the surface of Mars in 1976 found no life on Mars, but more recent probes have found that Mars was once a watery planet, and since water is a central building block of life as we understand it, the search for life is still on!

NEPTUNE: Oceans of incredibly cold liquid methane are what make Neptune shiny blue in color. Neptune also has the strongest winds in the solar system, blowing up to 700 miles per second, and a Great Dark Spot where storms whip up swirling clouds.

OBSERVATORY: Observatories are places where astronomers study space, using high-powered and massive telescopes. To give the best view of the night sky, most observatories are built on mountaintops far away from city lights.

PAYLOAD SPECIALIST: A payload specialist is a trained scientist who doesn't work for NASA but is a guest onboard a spacecraft. Payload specialists are trained by research or commercial organizations for specific space flights. A payload specialist is not necessarily a professional astronaut.

QUASARS: Quasars are the most intense source of light in the universe. They are as big as the solar system, and they are as bright as 100 galaxies! Quasars are the most distant objects known in the universe. Even the closest quasar is billions of light-years away.

ROCKET: Rockets provide the huge thrusts that are necessary to launch a spacecraft into space. The huge thrust is needed to beat the pull of Earth's gravity. Werner von Braun designed the first rocket capable of reaching space, the V-2 ballistic missile built by Germany in World War II. The most powerful rocket ever was the Saturn V, which sent astronauts to the moon during the Apollo program.

SATURN: Saturn is the second largest planet in the solar system. It is 815 times as big in volume as Earth. Saturn is known for its dramatic and beautiful rings. The rings are made up of millions of tiny, ice-coated rock fragments.

TELESCOPE: Telescopes magnify distant objects by using lenses or mirrors to bend light rays so they focus, or come together. Nowadays, most professional astronomers do not gaze at stars directly through a telescope. Instead, they rely on the visual and electronic data that telescopes from observatories collect for them.

U.S. MOON LANDING: The Apollo 11 was launched from the Kennedy Space Center on July 16, 1969 and on July 20, 1969, it made history when it landed on the moon. Aboard Apollo 11 were astronauts Neil Armstrong, Edwin E. "Buzz" Aldrin, and Michael Collins. Neil Armstrong was the first man to set foot on the moon and he said, "One small step for man, one giant leap for mankind." Millions of people watched the historic event on television.

VENUS: Venus has a thick atmosphere that reflects sunlight amazingly well and makes it shine like a star in the night sky. Venus is the brightest thing in the sky after the sun and the moon. Venus is sometimes called the "evening star" because it can be seen near the horizon just after sunset. It is also visible before sunrise because it is quite close to the sun.

WHITE DWARF STAR: Stars are hot and bright because of constant nuclear reactions. A white dwarf star is a star that has used up the fuel needed for these reactions. White dwarf stars are the last stage in the life of a medium-sized star. One of the few dwarf stars that we can see from Earth is a white dwarf star called Omicron-2 Eridani.

X-15: The X-15 was a high-speed aircraft used to provide information on thermal heating, high-speed control and stability, and atmospheric re-entry. Its first flight was in 1959. It holds both speed and altitude records for a winged aircraft. It reached a maximum speed of 4,534 miles per hour and an altitude of 67.08 miles.

YEAR: A calendar year is roughly the time it takes for the earth to travel once around the sun. Although a calendar year is 365 days, it actually takes the earth 365.24219 days to make its orbit, which is called a solar year. We add an extra day in February every four years to make up for this extra time. This is why we have leap year every four years!

ZENITH: The celestial sphere is an imaginary sphere with the earth at its center. It is used for describing the positions and motions of stars and other objects. The zenith is the point on the sphere directly above our heads as we look at the night sky.